Igor In Therapy

M. K. Garrison

Illustrated by Sarah Vosmus

Spuyten Duyvil
New York City

© 2021 M. K. Garrison
Etchings © 2021 Sarah Vosmus
ISBN 978-1-952419-67-6

Library of Congress Cataloging-in-Publication Data

Names: Garrison, Myah K., 2001- author.
Title: Igor in therapy / Myah K. Garrison ; illustrated by Sarah Vosmus.
Description: New York City : Spuyten Duyvil, [2021] |
Identifiers: LCCN 2021036096 | ISBN 9781952419676 (paperback)
Subjects: LCGFT: Poetry.
Classification: LCC PS3607.A77365 I36 2021 | DDC 811/.6--dc23
LC record available at https://lccn.loc.gov/2021036096

For my grandfather, Donald Dorsey,
who introduced me to black and white Hollywood horror movies;
I still think the effects are terrible but I admit I love them anyway.

Act One
A Well Remembered Hammer

*How convenient
that your best witness is dead.*

Confusion   now   hath   made   his   masterpiece.

*In the imperfect records left of the anatomy
of the ancient   Egyptians,
no trace
of any knowledge
of the spleen can be   ascertained.*

Scott Addams

William Shakespeare, *Macbeth*

Henry Gray

              "Let's start with green —
                    Can you picture it?
      Breathing and collapsing on the white tiles
      like Hollywood hemorrhaging its oldest effects.
                I stick my fingers in its stomach…
yank out whatever pearly string of information the Doctor wants.
              Why do dead monsters smell of turpentine?
                    Then, I burn the gloves
                    and down some ethyl alcohol."

I nod,
lean over my mahogany desk,
uncap fountain pen, ask his name.

                                                    "Igor."

He sits across from me
huddled in verdant coat,
shakes my hand.

                                                    "I think I
                                              may need therapy."

"The doctor wanted hip bones last night,
I pulled them from the ground
like weeds.
Rolled them up in a length of cotton,
carried home as a quiver
or kindling.
Cool breeze rifled my clothes —
fingers tapping in the dark.
cemetery was silent as a…"

Igor grins up at me,
hand flapping
to ward away his joke.

"The night was dry and starless.
I enjoyed the walk."

I ask if he likes work,
pencil balanced on lined paper.

"I'm fitted to it."

Cups his pointed chin between palms,
looks up
at ceiling…

"Have you met the Doctor?"

Black eyes twist my way,
curiosity frothing
round his pupils
.
.
.

Igor reclines
on my sand-colored couch,
right foot on floor.
I tell him no, never met the man.

"His hair is white.
Not old, younger than me. Still,
white hair."

I ask Igor what he hopes to find?
Lean forward; catalog his response.

> "There is no pocket of brilliance in my soul,
> no crazy heat burning up my hours
> in steel-stitched discovery
> but I have sense
> baked into this brain somewhere;
> I know how endless cremations
> and a bedroom full of pickled creatures —
> mal-formed limbs suspended in amber fluid —
> leads not to a healthy mind."

Igor frowns,
fingers tracing the ridge of his brow.

> "I am sloughing off insanity
> as swiftly as I'm able."

Head turns into the couch back,
face obscured in beige folds.
I stand, open window on
cold afternoon sunlight,
look across the village square;
haphazard spill of blocks.

"I bring him limbs, teeth,
yards of skin slowly turning yellow…
the Doctor is constructing."

Igor clenches his fist,
looks up as fingers unfurl.

He steps through the old oak door,
leans on empty bookcase —
fidgets across the room —
sits behind *my* desk.
.
.
.

I stand in front of Igor —
cross-armed, curious.

> "Exposed metal piping,
> strange electrodes buzzing,
> gaseous chemicals tainting
> my breath;
> understandable.
> I've cataloged every corroded valve,
> every
> half-alive creature."

Tosses a battered spiral-bound
journal towards me; crimson cover.
Pages of beautiful cursive,
line art,
lovely sketches of inside-out
monsters and long steel
instruments.

"A lump of flesh in the corner
of our lab.
Never twitches or squirms,
but it whispers
.
.
.
The Doctor will not tell me,
just sits, grinning by the thing.
I do not hate the grotesque,
I've clutched
a plethora of oozing creatures —
dissected
the hollow hearts
of every man
laid out over our
polished stone slab
.
.
.
Why now am I kept from his work?"

Igor enters to see a bat,
gliding as if by invisible string, through my office.
I balance on couch —
follow flapping with my eyes.
Tell Igor to open the window, voice high — full of
gaps.
He slides glass to the side,
stands with arms wide and useless.
The bat dives; I drop,
lay clutching at cushions.

                                                                                        "How did it get in?"

I shake my head,
rise, trip over the coffee table —
stand by Igor
.
.
.

The bat swoops low;
I can see veins that flow
like streams across its wings.

                                                                                        "Hate bats, always have."

Igor grips window edge,
I echo the sentiment.
Creature settles in a corner,
gazes wide eyed at us, ears twitching.
Igor grabs a pillow from the couch
before drawing a breath
and vaulting forward.
The bat boils across low ceiling;
bolts out window into sky.
I slam shut the glass, turn back —
gratitude stitched across soul.

                                                "Fifteen minutes late
to a half hour
session.
Sorry— old friends, angry mob,
and another twenty time-consuming
inconveniences."

Igor steps into my office, lips turning up
in half-observed mirth.
I put down paperwork,
smile as he sits on my couch,
ask what his friends said.

                                                "Married, children, divorced, dead—
we traded anecdotes, parted ways."

I nod, tell him I'm sorry for his loss.

                                                "She was the basketcase of our group,
don't be maudlin.
I remember her at twenty,
academic aspirations and violet hair.
Would not have approved of the Doctor.
She always thought I'd be working for her
one day."

Igor smiles at bare wall,
eyes distant, reflect lamplight.

"Explosion at the lab
yesterday,
pops of fuchsia sparks
tumbling
along copper wire
to nest in drywall."

I ask if he's hurt,
worry carving up my chest
.
.
.

Igor lifts a sleeve,
saffron cloth pulling away
to red welts, purpureal wrist.
He rolls his shirt back down,
sinks teeth to stop a grimace.

"I lifted twine-
bundled bones
in hot air,
carted boiling
jars of blood;
stuffed match-
boxes full of lashes
into my coat
pockets
.
.
.

                              The Doctor simply coaxed that creature
                                    he's created away from harm—
                                         sat, soothing it as I
                                           labored in flame."

Igor rolls his shirt sleeve up again,
sits tracing red marks with soot-stamped fingertips.

"The people in this village,
don't want any sort of brilliance
in their lives of assembly-line pottery,
half-baked chicken, soulless boots,
de-clawed family pets.
Not one of them could
stand my jars of cut-up tongue,
vats fizzing pink, or
barns stacked to the rafters
with radium —

.

.

.

How does life like that work?

.

.

I wire skulls with copper animation,
assist the Doctor in dark operations.
Since Fate doused
my dreams in formaldehyde —
Let me never be a baker,
a tailor, a lawyer, an engineer, a painter,
nothing in the world but discovery
and dizzying vapours."

My patient spills inked paper across my desk.
Look up into Igor's bright face;
he's early and sucking air.

                                            "Sorry, science scattering out
my ears. Liable to burst
if I don't
tell someone."

Igor taps the paper.
.
.
.

I pick up a sheet covered in little black
sketches of a man
walking, twisting,
sitting with a book balanced on his knee.

                                             "He can speak.
Low, whistling language —
gets vowels stuck in his teeth. Yesterday,
he sat by me,
and spoke of melting flesh;
rain, come to dissolve the very bones
we gave him.
Strange, hearing philosophy
from the halting tones of a
nascent man."

Sounds depressed, I observe.

                                                                   "A miracle!"

Shouts Igor. Arms wide,
and spinning.

> "It's alive! I'd never —
> were whispers speech?
> he kept breath a secret,
> hid the jumping heart.
> How could he knit bone without me
> finding the dregs?"

Igor paces; hands grasp
at invisible tools, peers over
an operation table —
full of animation.
A smile splits his face,
breathy exclamations of wonder
falling from pale lips.

> "The being can walk; shamble across
> lab floor.
> Can eat with a spoon, I fed it soup,
> tomato soup for our first creation.
> Spilled red on the smock we gave it."

Igor laughs, drawing hands through
his own black hair — dark falling
against flushed cheeks.

> "He has the touch!
> Life from bones and
> old pieces of skin.
> We are Gods
> .
> .
> .
> God,
> our Adam is gorgeous."

"Wanted to buy an orange.
Asked three shopkeeps and none
would sell to
me.
Am I so frightening?"

Igor curls his arm,
twists his lips in humor.
He lies back
on my couch, arm
still flexed above him.

Igor taps fingertips to thigh,
looks at me
like he can see a freight train
cutting quiet
to shreds of shrieking metal.

"The Miracle, our man,
heart stopped for four full minutes."

I see Igor bite the inside of his cheek.
Desk corner gouges
my palm, press into pain
to keep from
gasp.

"I resurrected him.
No indication as to why it happened."

"The village does not like our man.
Say he is stuffed with straw;
crude attempt at intimidation or
odd deity in second-hand skin.
Well, I've met their metaphor,
he has a voice, deep and gasping;
like his chest is full of flutter."

Looks over his
shoulder at me,
assuring that I follow.

He is sewn with lightning,
every seam a line of magic
made of surgical floss.
They've threatened him, us;
brought flames to our door."

Igor slams his arms against the couch
and does not
speak.

Igor sits on my couch,
back straight.
I hand over a mug of tea,
watch him breathe in steam.
Mint, I tell him.
He sips,
fingers twisting over warmth.
I watch from deep
within my scarlet armchair.
.
.
.

Smell of sawdust wafts around
our silence.
I ask how the doctor is.
Igor sets his mug down —
two inches from
leather coaster.
He reaches under
olive-colored coat —
draws out a book,
sets it on table;
paperback copy of
Prometheus Bound,
newly bought;

                                                    "For your shelf."

Motions to my bookshelf,
still bare from the move.
He leaves.

"This week has been stirring;
a pot near boil.
Villagers spit at me in the streets,
the Created man will no longer talk,
Doctor is frightened by quiet inaction.
Chaos gathers like a cloud
above us,
it must soon be swept off or
precipitate."

Igor rests against soft
couch, closes his eyes,
murmurs in a voice full of
red dust.

*"The very beams will dry those
vapours up,
For every cloud engenders not a storm.*
The bard said that; I hope
to believe him
when this tempest blows up or
over."

Igor smiles,
fog pushing part way
past eyes.
Dark curls fall
away from forehead — strange halo.

A shout scrapes
peace from our session.
Tall man
against the doorframe, arms braced.
He takes heavy breaths, sags
almost to kneeling.
White hair
falls
in strips down
his neck;
bleached, I observe,
roots are dark.
'The monster h-has
gone' says the man 'rioters attacked him
in the garden, he ran...ran out, across the moor.'
A stained lab coat hangs off his form, ripped at the arms.
.
.
.

Igor sits up,
eyes wide and black.

                                                                             "Doctor,
there is no rest
in the world anymore."

The man nods —
drops his head —
asks my patient to follow him.
.
.
.

Igor stands, slides on his jacket.
places a hand on the doctor's back.
I turn to the window.
In a minute
I can see the pair sprinting across the village square.

Igor holds his back; unnatural line.
Large green coat gathers around him;
mountain range of shadow and canvas.
He twists fingers into couch, gazing
at air
.
.
.

I ask what became of the creature,
my hands clasped in lap,
chin angled down.
Igor's eyes sweep over my shoulder.
He is wearing
a large knit hat; yellow.
Looks strange on his sallow self.

                                                "Edged out of this world."

Dead? I ask.

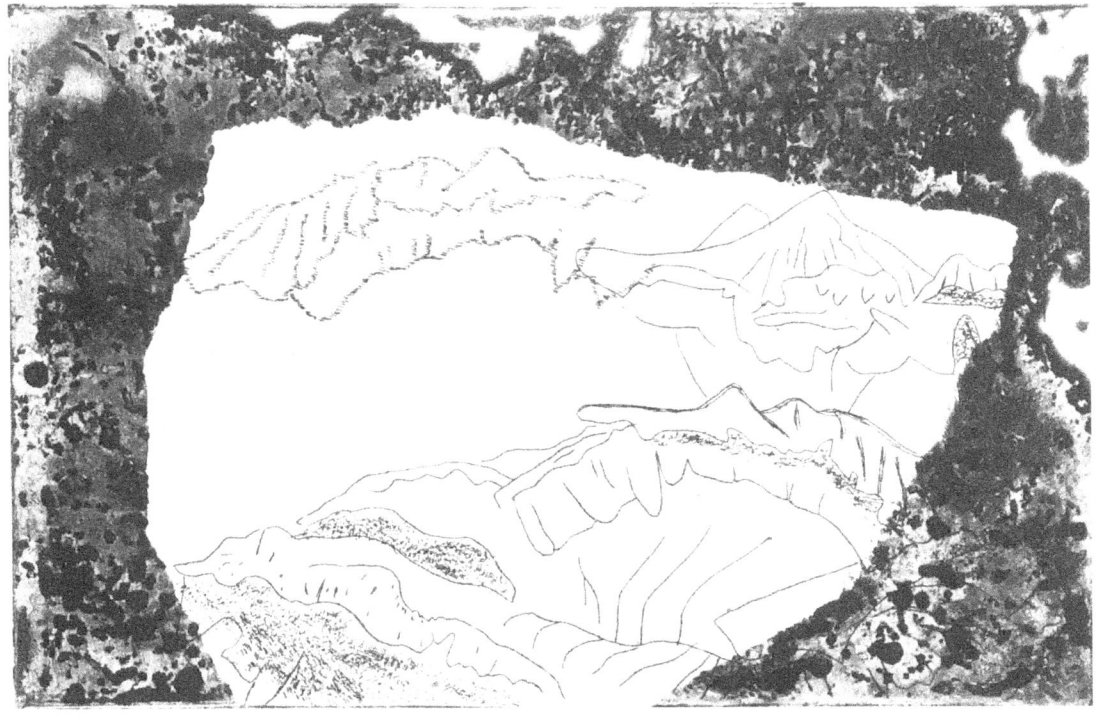

Act Two
Freud in a Moment of Innocence

The mere presence
of the idea was an   *irresistible*
proof of the fact.

you get up one day and somebody has
taken
one of the   *mountains away*

Could I   *create myself anew*
I would not fail   *in pleasing you.*

Mary Shelley, *Frankenstein*

Simon Armitage

Isaac Watts

Month of sitting in my office,
watching sunstreaks migrate sideways
across wood-paneled walls.
Igor does
not
step
through my door, does not even call.
I read the book he brought me
cry at appropriate parts.

"Never baked before."

Igor ducks his head as he walks into my office,
sidelong smile twisting up his chin.

"Yesterday I made bread,
can't live off takeout indefinitely.
.
.
.
The Doctor used to bake piles
of buttered rolls,
apple tarts, and tiny crescent cakes.
Said it was like mixing solvents
or shreds of organ in the lab;
intuitive to scientists.
I threw my attempt
into the woods where it billowed
up in smoke."

I laugh with Igor, forget to tell him
when the session ends.

Cold air
circles the room,
shifts a stack of paper on my desk.
I press palms
together, think on tawny blankets
tangled in my bed at home.

                                        "When I was young I wanted
                                                  to play the drums."

Warmth candles through my chest —
Ask if he still plays?

                                                        "Not for years.
                                          Used to have a band;
                                       Tony played the guitar —
                                            Just like a fist fight,
                                                some chap
                                          from Mullingar sang."

Igor shrugs, lips twitch;
he shivers,
skin raised to goose bumps.

                                              "Never any good,
I kept speeding up the rhythm
                     till at last the cymbals fell."

I bring Igor a cup of chamomile,
place it in his hands, curl his fingers,
lean back and chase his gaze.
Steam filters between us
like an animated pane of glass.

                                  "Threw out the Doctor's experiments.
                                      Don't think he's dead but —
                                            bubbled over tinctures
                                            reached expiration date,
                                              some sort of cosmic
                                            best-by time and I —"

Dark chuckle into mug.

                                            "Couldn't stand the smell."

Igor sits,
leans forward,
legs swing against my couch.
His hair is freshly cut;
smells of synthesized fruit.
I smile,
ask what went right?

> "College friends invited me to dinner.
> They read my article in *Bergman's*."

I start up from behind my desk,
pull a copy of *Bergman's* newest
from detritus by door.
Reaching out his arms, Igor grins,
finds page,
hums the absence of a melody
as I skim.

> "Exposé on electrical-organic animation."

Said in pompous projection.
I laugh, graze his shoulder.

I ask how dinner with friends was,
watch arms spread like oars over
the couch back.

                                                                       "Made up an excuse—
began incubation
of an artificial hound embryo;
dark outline
of amorphous matter
floating in liquid twilight."

Igor sits forward,
hands clutching elbows.
Wonder why—
he had been excited,
giddy, face flushed and bright as a quarter.

                                                              "Never meant to go,
just liked being asked."

Ask about the last time he had talked to
anyone other than me.

Door tips open and
spills
Igor
to floor.
I rise, offer an arm.

"Unborn dog flickering to life
in a test tube on my bookshelf
.
.
.
I created the creature,
stitched together several almost-lives —
submerged among electrodes.
Today I took it from the shelf
and watched blood
pump through hair-width veins."

Igor shifts, leaning
against the shut door of my office.
I fall back into gravity
behind mahogany desk.

"Tiny heart fluttering madly
beneath see-through flesh.
.
.
.
Won't last the night."

Corner of a smile,
Igor rubs a hand along his knee.

I ask how he handles an
empty lab?

.

.

.

Tap the desk, meet his eyes.
Igor walks the length of my office.

> "I read more, bible and bodice-rippers,
> try to mend that television
> I found in a ditch,
> and sometimes
> sit in silence."

I nod, open a window onto summer air;
scent of Gertrude Jekyll roses.

> "Strange,
> designing experiments alone.
> No one to check my notes,
> no sound,
> movement, thought,
> save those I orchestrate."

Patient joins me at the window,
looks out at red roofs.
There is a group in the square;
intoxicated folk songs

.

.

.

Igor kicks the wall,
suspires and collapses on my couch.

> "If nothing else, I miss *movement*."

Igor arrives ten minutes late,
plate of muffins
smoking in his arms.

"Took another try at baking.
Raspberry."

I pick one, feel the warmth
between palms.
Smell of baking soda wafts;
catches
on cobwebs in ceiling corners.

"Followed a recipe
the Doctor left, panicked when
I forgot vanilla but
edibility is all
I ask.
Puffed up in the oven
like I'd administered 'em
with helium."

Bite,
watch as steam pours
out of teeth-marks. Bland.
I thank him for the gift,
set the muffin on my desk,
down a swallow of tea.
Igor eats the rest inattentively
while we talk.

> "Hound embryo grows like a sponge soaks water,
> fattened and fluttering
> full of brand new biological structure.
> Everyday I expect to crack the casing,
> pour down drainage,
> but it just *keeps keeping*.
> I might stumble steps some morning,
> find it's birthed
> into a mess of leaping, sneezing pup."

Igor looks out at Sunday haze.
Arms curl around his chest,
draped in forest-colored coat.
Lips turn skyward,
mist collects on eyelids;
moisture migrating inward from open window.
I wonder if the dew on his cheek
used to be vapor or tears.

> "What co-
> lor do you
> think the eyes will be?"

I blank stare to Igor's left,
try not to dwell
on how his voice broke saying
color.

Igor seeps into my couch;
right arm thrown across his eyes,
left, dripping to the floor.

                                                  "—and I, I wonder how they walk."

Feet kick up,
fall.

                         "I see them— big bay-window in the lab—
                            tripping over frost-heaves on the street."

Ask if he's no longer a biped
like the rest of us? Pick up a pen,
twirl it like a baton.

                                                      "About motivation;
                                                         why move
                                   when you're headed towards
                                          teatime and joint pain?"

Watch Igor turn my way
before telling him
I've a box of Builder's tea in the back
and not every orbit spins around
a scientific center.
Igor lifts his left hand,
tilts fingers in admission.

                                              "No more glory in beakers
                                                  than brick laying."

Lets his head fall back against the couch,
smiles up at obscured sky.

We sit like conspirators; close and quiet.
Igor talks of the growing hound,
tells me about twitching muscle,
half-scooped eye sockets

.

.

.

Knuckles rap against door

.

.

.

Igor stands, green canvas swaddled round him;
pulled into gullies against skin.
A voice asks entry — spear in sudden silence.
Door cracks open like oblong egg,
emits a draggled and dredged-up man.

"Doctor? How have —
never seen your beard before."

The man pulls my patient's name from his lips
like a magician plucking scarves.
He scrambles across the room to us,
sets arms around his friend.

"I've thrown away your experiments;
putrid, wheezing as I poured
them into oblivion."

The doctor shakes his head,
white hair matted
around an ectoplasmic complexion,
before telling how their creation
'Ripped apart-t like tissue paper.'
Doctor grips his friend's shoulders,
draws him to the door.

                                                  "I will not be at our next appointment."

My hand waves, untrusting of speech.
Door swings shut — does not creek.

Through the office window,
I imagine a squat lab,
belching fumes from
twenty chimneys
.
.
.

Doors might be four-foot oak,
gold filigree painted on;
fishnet-stockings,
or padlocked apartment
plywood; doorbell
gagged by tape
.
.
.

I kick my desk.
Bored and parched,
no energy
to walk for water.

They arrive embroiled —
talk of DNA edits;
double helix twisting from lips
In an odd lattice of punnett verdicts.
The doctor shakes my hand, says he'll *'pay extra*
if I allow him in the ses-s-sion.'

.

.

.

Tilt my head, ask if he agrees.
Igor nods, slips sideways on my couch; no room
for his employer.
I step behind my desk
and watch the doctor sink to floor.

                                  "The created man unstitched
                       somewhere north of vegetation, surrounded
                            by sunlit ice and powdered sea.
                                  The Doctor tells me
                          air was cold enough to freeze spit.
                              I doubt our art even noticed
                                       the temperature
                                              drop."

I ask how he feels,
knowing the first man-made-man
is dead. Watch as Igor
stretches arms above head,
green coat splayed by his sides
like a pair of crumpled wings.

                                         "I want to build another."

The doctor extends his legs
across my floor, then smiles...

I find the doctor a chair,
small wicker thing my mother left me.
Sit in my own red wingback —
watch the two
babble out equations.
Igor looks at me,
taps the doctor's scalp.

"Met my college friends
last night. Left early,
glass of beer half-drunk,
enjoyed the company.
Edward became an actor
and a waiter.
Invited me to an
interpretive dance production
of *Oedipus Rex*."

I grimace, touch
pen to my wrist,
ask if he intends to attend?

Igor enters with arms a rounded cradle,
green coat bunched about midriff.
The doctor follows into my office,
lab coat hanging off his form; excess of cloth.

                        "Already has a coat of black curls.
                                  Two AM this morning
.
.
.
                  I lay unconscious in the lab. Incubator blared alarm,
              Red light flooded the room, felt like our house was aflame
                              again. Ten minutes and she was awake,
                    could walk in twenty, paws don't have much traction
                            on rose-patterned linoleum floors."

Igor sits next to my desk, opens his arms.
A little mop of fur spills onto floor, stands, wobbles.
Dog blinks and wags her tail frantically.
I smile, crouch down to join the happy pup,
ask if she has a name.
Igor lets himself slip,
legs splayed; form a barrier.

                                            "I call her Rex."

The doctor tilts his chin earth-ward, smiles wide. I
scratch Rex behind her ear and say nothing.

Igor steps into the square
as I prepare to leave.
Window open to the town's noise,
I hear my patient talking
about percentage-
chance of organ failure
in any particular individual;
running through
mathematical probabilities
as he tosses a ball
for his week-old dog.

Act Three
Phrenology as Fallacy

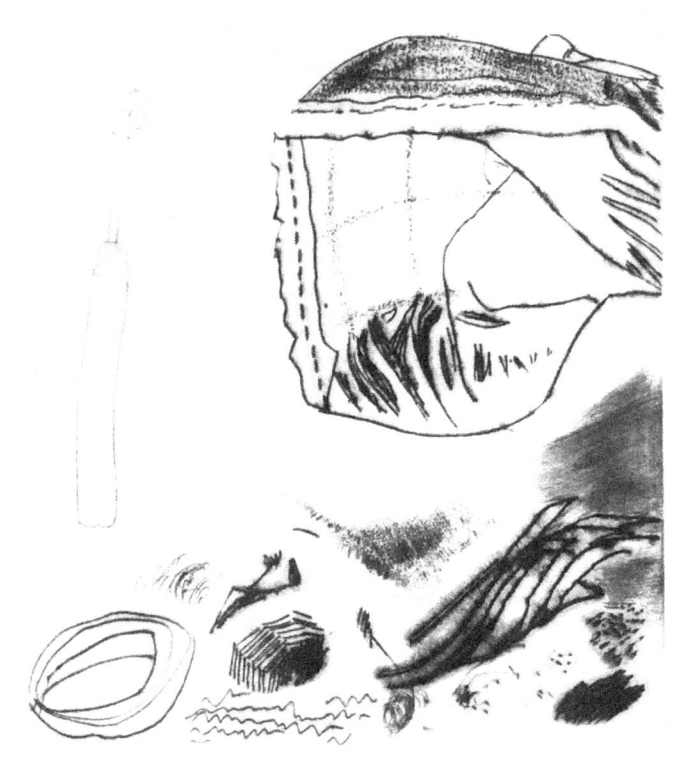

My life has been full of terrible misfortunes most of which never happened.

you got to remember that a worm, with very few exceptions, is not a human being.

My own self - consciousness cries out to me coldly: how does one love zero?

Michel De Montegine

Young Frankenstein

Auguste Villiers de l'Isle-Adam, *Tomorrow's Eve*

"We built a box of glass,
edged with steel.
Doctor stayed up all night,
mixing powder and gelatinous cubes;
melted into scarlet soup."

Igor presses palms to his forehead
an inch above eyes,
fingers splay out like the sun.
The doctor is a rough-hewn statue.

"I told the Doctor
that Rex was grown, unlike
the man; latched together
as house-siding and—"

Quick look to his employer,
sitting straight in wicker chair.

"He flew through motion
like a stone tossed
out into gravity."

The doctor enters alone.
Eyebrows, collar, cheek, tinged with sky
and I wonder if he feels frozen?
He tells me *'Igor is gone to the morgue;*
tourist not r-resident.'
—said quickly, hand outstretched, apologetic.
He sits on the wicker chair,
considers,
moves to couch.
I ask why he has come to therapy?
.
.
.

The doctor tells me he has *'a problem with the color green.'*
I lean back and look out my window, see
barely pink flowers, more leaf than bud.
'Glass box is full of liquid, vibration, pops of...of light,
and a nearly non-existent h-h-human embryo—
pulled together scraps of cells'
says the doctor,
voice low and quiet.
'It's growing, expanding, functioning
and Igor is its imp-impetus'
.
.
.

The doctor tells me of an
'itch to upset the whole casing,
t-take a baseball bat
to glass
and watch
amber liquid rush away,
across tiled floor'

.
.
.
I ask why it bothers him
his friend is brilliant,
take time to straighten a pad of paper
on my desk.
The doctor presses his lips together,
mouth flatlining through the session.

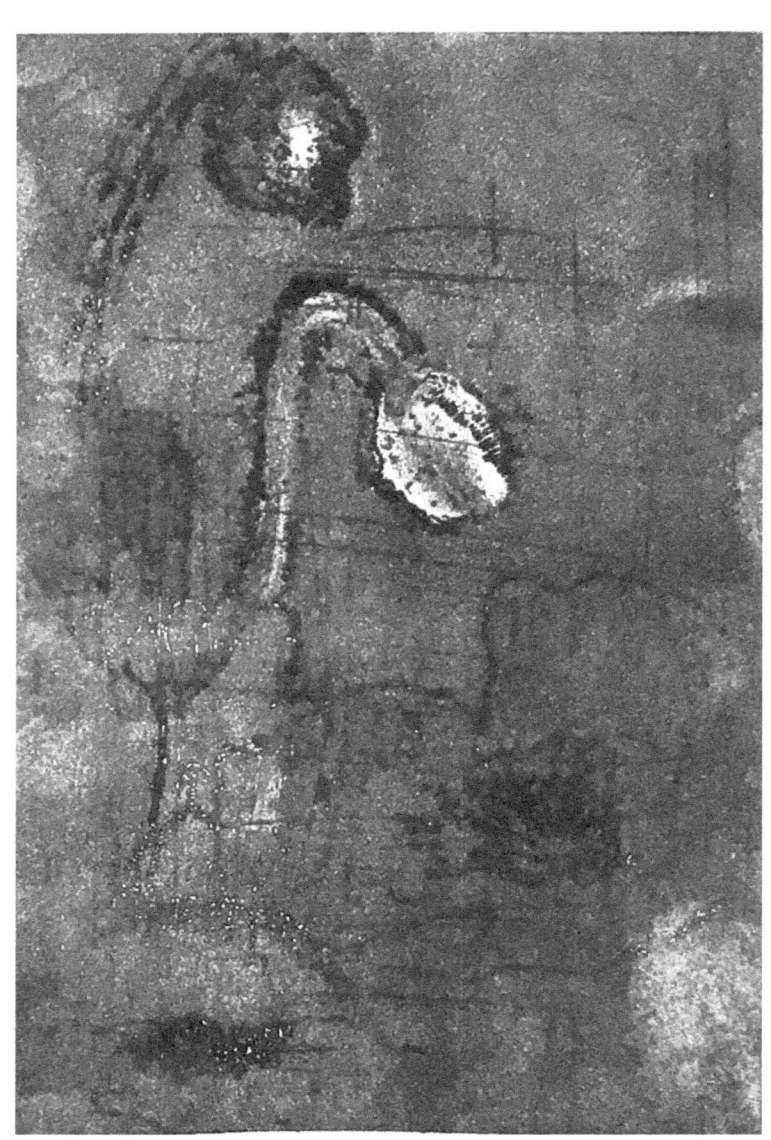

                                                       "Came home from morgue,
hauling two pillowcases full of

.

.

.

well that's not

.

.

.

The Doctor was curled up in a shadow,
barely raised his forehead from desk.
Spoke like a case of liquor."

Igor is alone, no dog, no boss.
Cold air drips from form;
ice bleeds into drink.

.

.

.

Toss him a copy of *Bergman's*,
new article authored by Igor,
ask to be told if he's published again

.

.

.

he tips his head forward and laughs through chest
like a ghost appearing at garden wall.

Igor arrives in a
hot huff of wind;
some desert god crawls
behind him; skinning knees
to clutch my patient's heels
with sharp fingertips.

"Nothing about summer is useful.
Too hot, too bright,
too humid —
can't think when
the air is more
dew than breath."

He sits, drops head; a plate
shatters into cupped hands.

"The Doctor canceled our subscription."

Igor stands in my doorway,
left hand holding Rex back
from rushing room.
He is without green coat;
oak plucked of leaves.

"*Bergman's*. I mean. May I?"

I nod and grab a hold of Rex
as Igor skims flayed lung
and bisected bones flutter
past his eyes
like pinned
insect wings

.

.

.

Igor slips
shut the magazine,
stares wide-eyed and empty.
I pet his dog.

"I am a gardener now

.

.

.

The Doctor has me tending tomatoes,
digging potato graves and hanging peas

.

.

.

He sits in front of the fish-tank-turned-womb
scratching out lines with his horrible hand

.

.

.

I bring him coffee, or scarlet bell peppers."

> "*'Let your plans be dark
> and impenetrable as night, and
> when you move, fall
> like a thunderbolt'*
>
> .
>
> .
>
> .
>
> Sun
> Tzu, on the lips
> of my employer"

Igor kicks his feet against hardwood floor,
tilts forward, and gesticulates
like an actor over-shooting.

> "I'll have no shrift with it.
> Bits of broken lightbulb
> meld with my skin, reflect dimly
> against ego, flicker out
> with the storm;
> This deluge swamps my chest —
> liquid rust come to choke a reservoir.
> Lies and averted eyes
> make my stomach burn."

I stare at my shelves,
sans book, save
the one Igor had given me,
and think of buying in bulk
with no intent to read.
Unopened books border on heresy
but an empty shelf,
like a ship perched
—parched for sea—
has always inspired
my soul to drip
with sympathy. Igor
does not swing open
my door, does call, says—
safe, and sorry.
I leave early.

Huddled into couch-corner,
Igor is crying;
no attempt to brush
water from his face.
I rock forward in my chair, watch
with awe curling across brain,
the way sugar spindles through water.
.
.
.

I ask
but he does not hear.

"The being in the glass case,
it grows, will soon be all accounted for.
Not at all like creating Rex.
Somehow its fingers;
twitching into amber,
and its nose
.
.
.

Never before seen beauty in the arch of a nose.
Every aspect of this person
seems perfection made of bones.
We had only some dust and a chalk-outline to follow
but no scientist, no artist, no human on this earth
could create a thing more worthy of our world.
.
.
.

I am plagued by odd associations;
I see our creation in a peony's curving petals,
color contrast of a shell on sand,
equal steps of a pinecone,
and great mountains carved into star-strung sky
.
.
.

How flawed the Doctor and I are,
how rough and laughable
next to this thing we have wrought.
We are as snakes stealing angels;
dragging heaven backwards, like a sheet,
to walk in squalor beside us.
I am too full of greed
to wish this being back into non existence,
but I cannot imagine we deserve it."

Igor smiles, I ask about his day.
Someone slugged the doctor.
Look up, see Igor bite on laugh.
Set my pen down.

> "I, in the garden, untangling vine
> heard a knock.
> Doctor opened door,
> lab coat still singed from...
> Tony, fourteen months a father,
> asked to see me.
> A muffled fuss—
> someone decided to be witty.
> Doctor tried to close door,
> I left garden to see
> Tony sock him;
> bled more than the dead.
> A few friends dragged Tony away,
> feet left tracks in the dust."

Igor tilts, and stretches across
my couch like a cat after catch.

> "I took the Doctor to a clinic,
> but no one would treat him."

Ask if Igor met his friends?
sip mint tea, watch him pick a book
from my newly crowded shelves.
Igor runs a finger over blue-cloth cover,
gold print hid by skin.

"Wedding last weekend.
found an un-bloodied shirt and congratulated
the couple. Hadn't met the groom before;
close cut hair, coin cufflinks,
yellow contact lenses?"

Igor puts my book down,
wanders to the room's center.

"Bride's named Lucy, wrote a few papers
on phosphorescent ferns. Helped me research
respiratory failure some summers ago.
Odd, when friends marry, no one in
the world deserves Lucy, still…"

He turns to me, smile sliding leftward.

"I wouldn't inflict her
on anyone halfway decent."

Crimson, spiral bound,
splays across
Igor's lap,
paper turns like ship sails tacking
as he flips through

.

.

.

Cursive loops in lines of notation;
'strange chicken'
'collected cobalt stones'
'twenty four finger-nails' catch my eye
and pull me forward.

                                        "One more week, perhaps two."

Igors rips a page from his book,
holds wrinkled paper out to me.

                             "She has grown faster than most embryos.
                                 Suppose we gave her a head start."

Graphite impressions
of tiny fingers, hairless head, tightly shut eyes.
I smile, say I'd love to meet her

.

.

.

Igor nods, rubs a hand
across his forehead.

The doctor knocks ten minutes before
Igor is set to. I put down my book,
do not stand.
Door shuts; clasp of a casket.
He sits, lab coat shot through,
see my desert-colored couch past tiny tears.
The doctor hunches forward,
head rise, open eyes.
Lips like chips of ice;
light-blue frost barring speech

.
.
.

The doctor clasps hands around his knee,
says *'Igor has published again,*
received an a-award, a grant.
Bergman wants him
to give a speech.
I'd like to be proud, am proud,
still feels like a lungful of cot-t-ton wadding.'

.
.
.

Door slips open —
Igor falls into my office like a crash of water,
draft catches clothes, limbs, caterwall of speech.
Rex runs silent circles,
never yet heard her bark.

"Can't speak with you today.
She is about to be born,
our moulded marble.
You should see her;
hair splayed inside the liquid like brushstrokes
and when she moves her eyelids — Doctor?"

The doctor lets slip a breath,
turns, sliding sideways:
*'Must go, t-thank you,
and all that.'*
Exeunt drains room of motion. Door slams.
All is colourless, silent, still.

Slide fingers over polished desk.
Hadn't expected Igor.
.
.
.

Gulp the last of my tea—
turn mug upside down over old notes.

Chase fly across office;
grey dot — body barely out of reach.
Out-stretched flail then I sit.
Insect hovers over white walls;
pencil mark I can't erase.
Shift
eyes through window,
disown the speck.
Town green is deserted.
Palm on chilled glass,
try to pick out any
one person.

I stretch out across couch.
This will be the third appointment missed.
Eyes shut, feel sunlight inch up arm;
warm air smells of honey.
Press forehead against soft upholstery,
and melt among cushions.
Unfurl an origami crease of Idle thoughts
.
.
.
Sound like sky-rip
beats black and blue my reverie.
I turn over as aftershocks echo.
Stand, rush window, see a
peak of sparks, white-edged flame,
hugging house on the edge of town.
Blast of yellow heat
pushes roof apart;
rips glass from frame.
Smoke boils above in black knots,
streaming out over rooftops.
People crowd the scene in a mess
of masked faces brandishing torches.
I shut my window,
falter out into street.

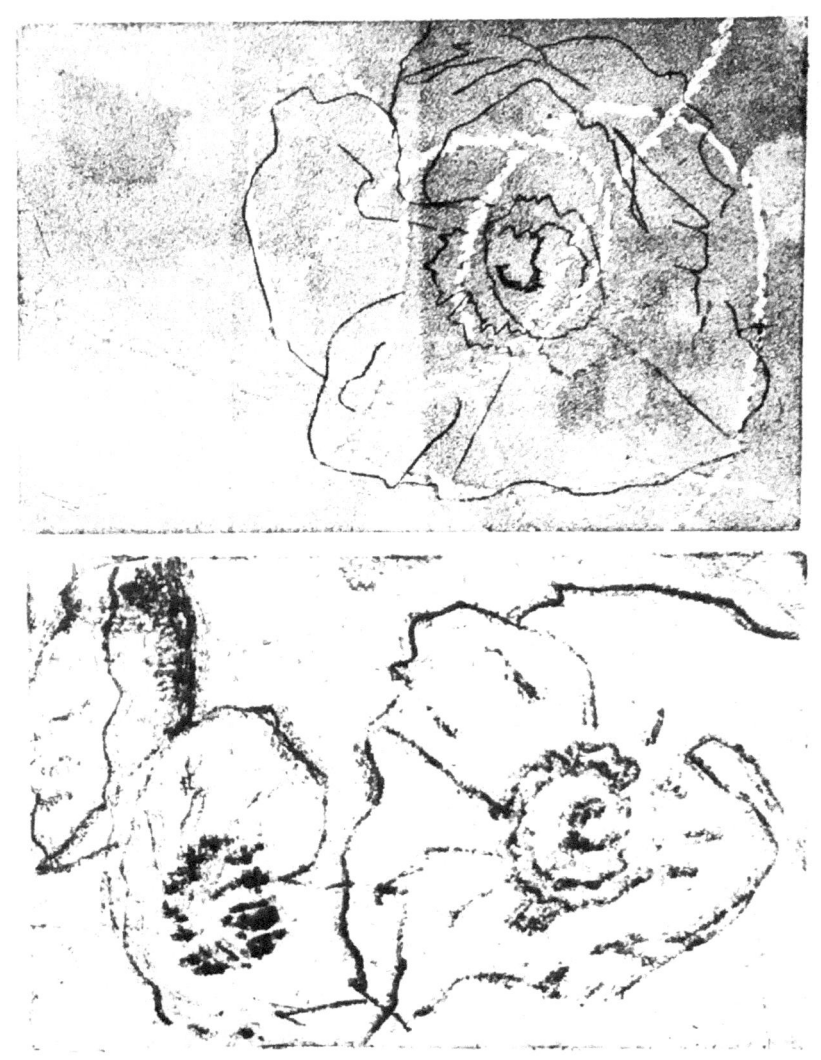

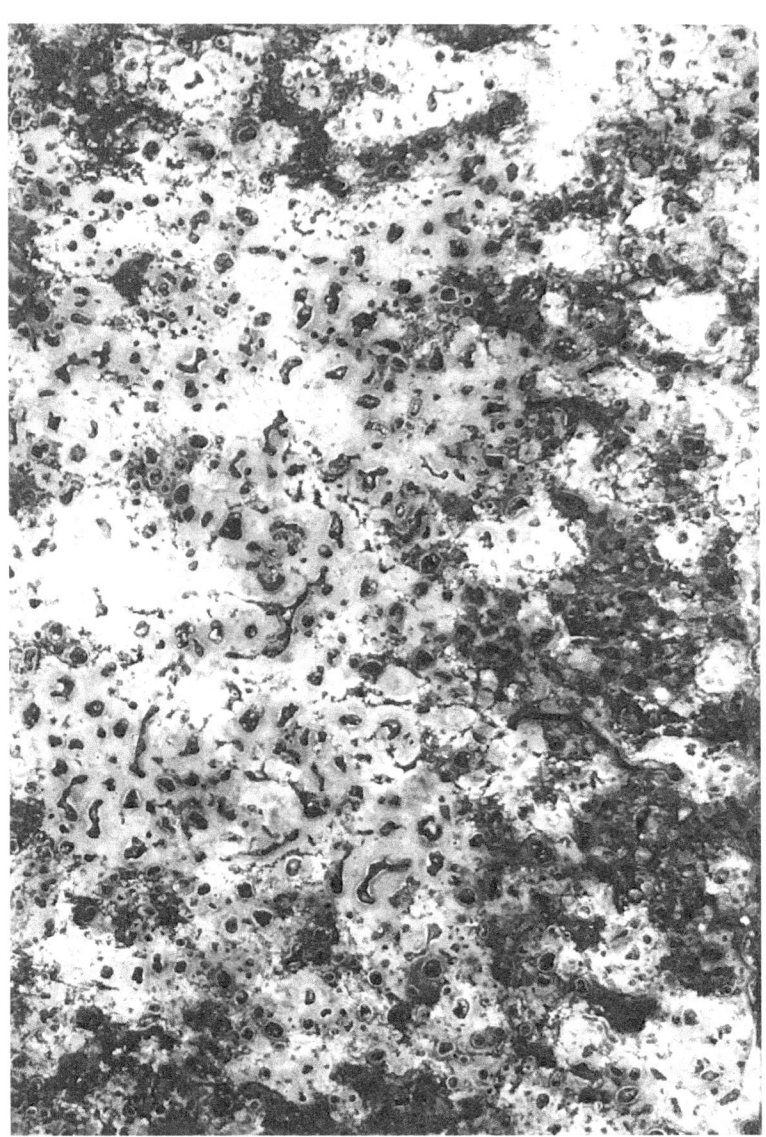

Act Four
A Forgotten Fire Bucket

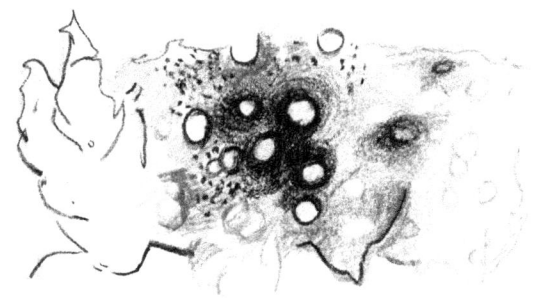

I sometimes think we must be all mad and that we shall wake to sanity in strait-waistcoats.

Some Roomba units can adapt to perform other, More creative tasks,

...one morning, without having done anything truly wrong, he was arrested.

Bram Stoker, *Dracula*

Wikipedia: Roomba

Franz Kafka, *The Trial*

Igor enters unkempt and angry.
I stand, ask if he is alright.

> "Villagers want us gone;
> came leaping like fleas across our fence,
> scratching at windows.
> Fumbled a box into our kitchen,
> lit the fuse and left.
>
> .
> .
> .
>
> Lucky the Doctor was out,
> lucky he had the child,
> lucky I left when I saw the box
> tumbling across our floor."

He falls like lead onto the couch
and looks at me.

Igor and the doctor arrive together,
sit side by side on my couch.
I tilt forward, ask how they have been?

> "We are the artists of her emboly,
> arranged tissue,
> chose color in each iris,
> placed every atom of her genesis."

Fullmoon of a face
unveils from Igor's green coat.
Dark eyes gaze at air,
tiny mouth stretches in toothless gap,
and the three of us smile.
Infant reaches hand out of warmth,
closes fingers around the coat-button.

> "Took a day to name her; hadn't
> realized she'd need one.
> Madeleine; heroine of some
> dogeared book I spent two pennies on,
> thought it a nice sort of sound."

Madeleine inhales with unexpected force,
begins to cry.
The doctor unfurls a finger
to touch her nose.

"I know exact width of her fingernails,
rhythm of blood, volume in each lung.
New rage pulling at my every beat to understand
with scientific certainty what little pressure is needed
to tear her skin.
Doctor and I, we log each exhale,
blinks, nonsense movement of her lips.
I read notes on her breathing pattern
before breakfast.
Can't sleep for the statistical possibility
of shuttered throat,
overzealous cells."

The doctor drags Rex in by collar.
Dog crouches low, worries her paw.
'H-heard the mob,
metal meeting metal, rush of thumps,
shouted words, she got s-s-scared.'
The doctor mutters, lips pulling taught.
Igor's eyes fall shut.
Madeleine; wrapped within his arms.

"Crowd of covered faces outside
the two-room we've rented.
They wear masks;
anonymous atrocities.
Wonder what number of
eyes I'd recognise."

Baby huffs breath, eyes blown wide.
The doctor pulls her to his lap, looks up,
''They are… are angry at our parroting of god.
Hallucinate weapons where we
h-hold our paintbrush.'

"Guns do not breathe.
Doctor and I poured
blood and bone into Madeleine,
humanity won't be unwoven from
her DNA."

The doctor smiles, runs a hand
through newborn's wispy hair.

Watch the two scientists from behind my desk.
They pass mathematical equations
like a cigar, dragging strings
of numerical conjecture
instead of white smoke.
Madeleine grabs at the doctor's fingers
as he calculates how many heart beats
he has left.
Igor laughs,
mumbles a word on reanimation,
and sips green tea newly brewed.
.
.
.

The doctor steps towards my book case;
'A collection of Bergman's,
m-may I?'
He takes the latest, runs an index finger down
table of contents.
'Igor, c-conference lists you
as top speaker
congratulations, and all that…'
Igor nods, tight,
downward,
smile.

Igor enters like a diving falcon,
all alone, abrupt, and awkward limbs.
Set my mug down, watch
him through silver hangings.

                                  "Said *congratulations*. Said
                                     he'd come, see me *speak*.
                             Spent the last year pulling
                                         me out of importance

                                                   .
                                                   .
                                                   .

                              No neural nets for men such as
                                           I. Couldn't let me
near powdered poison — might inhale.
                                  Now he wants to attend?

                                                   .
                                                   .
                                                   .

                              No, wrench femurs from graves,
                              pull potatoes out our garden;
                                    dust and earthworms;
                                    all you are allowed."

Attention drips out Igor's skull,
pools into fingers, falls like rain around him.

"Our rented rooms are empty,
food stacked in ragged boxes by door,
two unmade beds, crib...
Need to trip over froth filled tubs
of green, table towered with skinless fingers,
or hear the whine of kerosene."

Ask if Madeleine is doing well,
pace to window, open onto scrunched
faces. Say; *They're holding signs*.

"I've enough press for election;
public disgust and arrogant artistry.
Bill myself as mad man
with a god-complex."

Igor grins, rubs a hand along
the sharp bone of his chin.

"Madeleine is a happy child.
Damn the Doctor, but he
makes sure of her contentment."

The doctor asks to wait for Igor.
I nod, grind teeth,
let Madeleine wrap her hand around my finger.
Ask if he knows Igor is… competent?
The doctor's lab coat drapes like marble across back.
He nods. *'Chemical reactions in ev-very*
ounce of my b-blood. My soul is full
of invention, bone density,
or a mountain of white sparks.
Igor spent four years burning fact into the back of his head
between c-crystal pillars. I could not let him
outstrip my art with bought brilliance.'
The doctor cradles Madeleine closer to his chest,
lets her pull coat collar, turns, says —
'I plan, sketch, aspire, but without
him it's akin to shaping mist.
He will not let me thank h-him.'
The doctor's eyes slide left of ear.
I put pen to paper. Door jumps open and —

> "Doctor... I thought you
> were fitting metal pipes together?"

The doctor rises like sea surf,
says, *'Throng of people coming back from the store,*
hit flat of my back with a shovel,
aiming f-for Madeleine.'

Couch askew.
Igor, stretched like a chalk-outline
over floor. I gaze down from my desk.

"No qualms with playing god;
give me
the lightning rod, host of angels.
Still, scratched out, spray painted, judge ruling
brings the thought of Madeleine back
to me. What becomes of her?
Bladed on cold altar?
Seize and crumple like a paper cup
being squeezed?"

I ensnare my throat,
fingers touching vocal chords.
Stare through yellow haze at Igor
sketching horror through his child's future.

"Perhaps... I *am* Icarus,
the Doctor and I certainly scratched the sky-
brought it down like a pain of glass
shattering across our backs.
Will Madeleine melt?"

I sit alone, stare endless at page;
Igor hasn't come.
Breathe, bored gaze
at a book I bought with
the intention of being changed
in some cosmic,
red sky,
soul screaming,
sort of way.
Put the purchased passion away;
find I've forgotten title.
Stretch arms out across desk.
Press my cheek into sun
warmed wood.
Strange how a patient
becomes a story —
men such as them
must bathe in fire.

Igor talks of college;
twists fingers through green.
Stripe of sunlight licks across office,
gilds his cheek.
Door swings open

.

.

.

The doctor stands straight and thin,
looks at Igor; paper plate face
ready to crumble in ash.

                                                                                  "Deja vu Doctor?"

'Villagers-s pulled her from my arms.
Opened eyes hours after. Don't
know w-where…'
Igor leaps to standing,
walks like ruin

.

.

.

The doctor pushes
a hand into Igor's shoulder,
confesses *'S-sorry, You are no…*
no near-drained lab assistant,
come to cut corners,
ogle bottled eyes.
You are more than half of ev-v-very
experiment I have d-done, every action I take.'

.

.

.

The two men stay
a second.
Igor nods, says something hushed
and hurried as they leave.

Phone rings, shatters vision,
clapping hands — golden chalice.
Pick up, spin chair and ask
what I can do?

"Won't be able to attend therapy
today. This is Igor by the way"

Static buzzes,
press head close, ask
if his daughter is ok?

"Can't sleep for seeing fist
slung through the dry skeletons
of those who took Madeleine;
disperse as dust
born away by breeze.
.
.
.

Absence feels like someone
took scissors to my chest —
left skin and trembling empty
to miss her."

Open lips to reassure-
dial tone spears through morning mist
to the point of green visibility.

Soft air pillows skin.
Open window bleeds wind
through office.
I snag
sight on frothing crowd
boiling around a bundle,
held low
as they infest a house
.
.
.

Puff breath
Into—
Nothing
.
.
.

Pick up the
phone.

Stand square
at window—
two men run
through town's center.
The doctor spins; steel reflecting sun,
looks up. Gape my
jaw, point.
.
.
.
Green jacket grabs
at the doctor—
knocks loose paint off
red door.
.
.
.
Igor hands strip of cloth to—
ties another across
tooth-filled mouth.
Door pulls inward— black.
.
.
.
Small sphere falls
from fingers of the scientists,
propels forward— splits
yellow smoke. Streaks
of vapor pour across square,
fill sky. I smell sulfur,
shut window,
sit down.

Drift of yellow smoke curls my ankle; drift of pungent air sleeps on my chest
.
.
.
Into dust and newly rended fabric; into the chapel of Artemis
.
.
.
Eyes edge over the window ledge, eyes stink and itch in odd air
.
.
.
I see Igor like a flame-cast marionette. I duck below the ledge of
.
.
.
my desk. Hear the crack of fire; hear pound of my own pulse
.
.
.
Red sparks staircasing into sky; red beads my arm where I bite down.

I sit cross legged on my desk,
drink too-hot tea, watch dust fall
through a column of light.
Door opens,
slide quickly to feet.

"Baker nearly bit me
when I bought a loaf today."

Igor grins, puts his hand
out, stills midair.

"Madeleine is alright, only a little
distressed. Wish I possessed the courage
of those too young to know."

The doctor stands to side,
thanks me. I nod,
gesture to window,
thumb a line
along my spinal-cord.
We three sit down to talk.

                                "Some kid smashed our windows last night."

The doctor chuckles, folds coat
over the back of my couch.

                                "Lucky Madeleine wasn't there,
                    I've enough acid to melt the man down a drain —
                            would in a beat, if he touched her."

I ask where she was,
push pen to desk's edge
where it wobbles like a weathervane.

                                        "Tony took her, she's safe."

I look to the doctor who shrugs,
presses a palm to his forehead;
sinner waking
halfway through a sermon.

I open door, smile
down at Madeleine as she
reaches
up.

                                            "Thought to bring you another book,
                                            but I doubt there's room anymore.
.
.
.
.
                                                  Thank you, few are fine
                                                        with flames
                                                    and the moving dead."

Touch Igor's sleeve,
tell my friend
to publish more, I like his words.
.
.
.

The doctor shakes my hand,
takes her out of Igor's arms.

                                      "She will be walking in several months.
                                          Formaldehyde, copper, and calcium
.
.
.
                               I couldn't even tell you how we managed it."

Igor shrugs at me, eyes wide.
.
.

The doctor holds door
as they exit
my office in rush
of billowing bright lab coat;
reminds me of smoke.

The End

It   sits   there
looking   at me;
and I don't know what it is.

. . .

a thousand thousand slimy things lived on;
and so did
I.

Everything is more beautiful
because   we're doomed. You will never be lovelier
than you are now.
We   will never   be here again.

Star Trek: The Next Generation, "Measure of a Man"

Samuel Taylor Coleridge, "The Rime of the Ancient Mariner"

Homer, *The Iliad*

A letter received by
W. I. Jørgensen counseling
on November 8th   --

         Pollen   presses soft
       Against   my   skin.
    I am unknowable   in   a   field   of   purple
   Unwanted   by   the   sky   but   perfectly
                                                              Content
 To   love   whatever dirtied   stretch of smoothness   I am allowed.
   You   never saw me like this.
  Never knew that I could sigh my   breath away into gold vapors
 And close my eyes against all that is not bright as the   thumb printed sky.

                                                                   .   .   .

   Trees   were smoking with pollen, and my hair was rising in the wind,
 When the doctor said "I do believe, it's the end."   blinking at cattle
    As they roamed,   listless,   round the daisies.
   He raised a   branch
  From   the   pebbled   ground   and   threw   it among tall grass.
 "The   cows   won't   hurt   you."
 I said,   wrinkling my nose
  Into   the   gusting   north.
 "I mean the work."   the doctor told me,
 Turning   and   heading   towards   the   farm   house.
 "Nothing   is   ever   the   same   once you have seen the peaceful
Life   of   milk   cows."

                                      —Your friend, Igor

Acknowledgements

Heather Woods, whose edits, mentorship, and good humor I have been exceedingly lucky to know.

Sarah Vosmus, whose art added so much to this book.

My parents, whose support and ability to actually spell words I have ever availed myself of.

Ava Teegarden and Aneile Holtrop who edited an early draft of this work and offered much encouragement.

Grace Sanford, my long-suffering friend, whose encouragement and insightful comments helped develop this work.

Finn Dierks-Brown and Charles VanWest, who read this piece aloud for me which was incredibly helpful.

David Sloan and his 2020 Poetry class, which critiqued a two-page version of this book with much more enthusiasm than the piece deserved.

Louanne Robinson, who helped me in making the therapy sessions more realistic.

Hooper, my cat, whose contributions to this work can not *possibly* be understated.

Ava Teegarden

M. K. Garrison is a poet and short story author living in Southern Maine. Her work has appeared in several local magazines including *The Portland Press Herald*, *Gen Z*, and the *Maine Women's Magazine*. She is a recent graduate of Maine Coast Waldorf School and will be attending Bennington College where she hopes to continue her studies in both prose and verse. M. K. Garrison lives with her parents, two dogs, a cat, six chickens, a goose, and a goat, all of whom are very supportive except, perhaps, the goose.

Sarah Vosmus received an MFA in printmaking from the University of New Mexico, she took her first printmaking class while studying abroad in NSW, Australia. She is a member of Circling the Square Fine Art Press and Co-Owner of a small letterpress shop. Sarah Vosmus is currently an adjunct lecturer at the University of Maine in Augusta, and exhibits her work nationally and internationally.

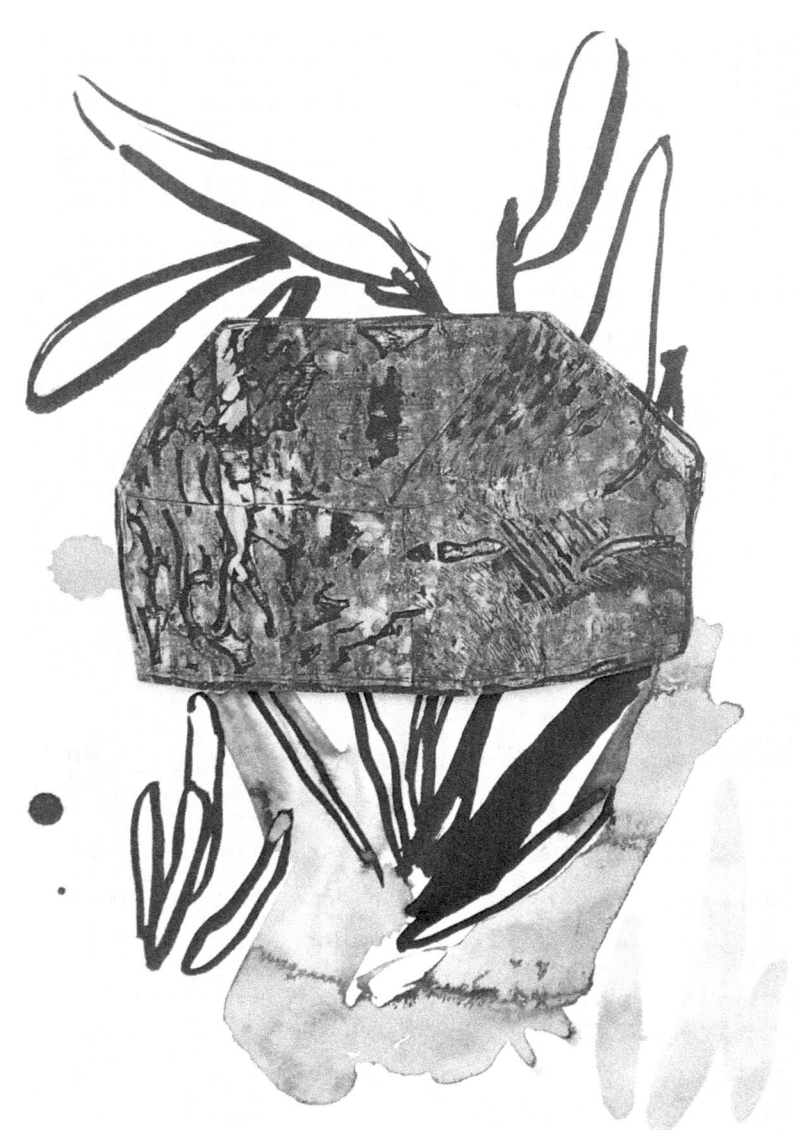

www.ingramcontent.com/pod-product-compliance
Lightning Source LLC
Chambersburg PA
CBHW081750100526
44592CB00015B/2365